S0-BRD-461

Predators in the Wild

Hawks

by Kathleen W. Deady

Consultant:
Dr. George F. Barrowclough
Department of Ornithology
American Museum of Natural History
New York, New York

CAPSTONE
HIGH-INTEREST
BOOKS

an imprint of Capstone Press
Mankato, Minnesota

Capstone High-Interest Books are published by Capstone Press
151 Good Counsel Drive, P.O. Box 669, Mankato, Minnesota 56002
http://www.capstone-press.com

Library of Congress Cataloging-in-Publication Data
Deady, Kathleen W.
     Hawks/by Kathleen W. Deady.
     p. cm.—(Predators in the wild)
     Includes bibliographical references and index (p. 32).
     Summary: Describes hawks, their habits, where they live, their hunting
methods, and how they exist in the world of people.
     ISBN 0-7368-1064-1
     1. Hawks—Juvenile literature. [1. Hawks.] I. Title. II. Series.
QL696.F32 D42 2002
598.9'44—dc21
                                                          2001002926

Editorial Credits
Blake Hoena, editor; Karen Risch, product planning editor; Timothy Halldin,
     cover designer and illustrator; Katy Kudela, photo researcher

Photo Credits
Ann & Rob Simpson, cover
Greg W. Lasley/KAC Productions, 17 (top left), 24, 27
Joe McDonald, 12
Joe McDonald/TOM STACK & ASSOCIATES, 10, 29
Kent and Donna Dannen, 14
Mark Newman/Photo Network, 17 (bottom right)
Rick Hobbs, 16
Robert McCaw, 11, 15, 17 (top right), 18, 20, 21
Rob Simpson/Visuals Unlimited (bottom left)
Stephen J. Lang/Visuals Unlimited, 9, 22
Unicorn Stock Photos/Robert E. Barber, 6; Dede Gilman, 8

1 2 3 4 5 6 07 06 05 04 03 02

Table of Contents

Features

Fast Facts

Common names: Hawk, bird of prey, raptor

Scientific names: There are several hawk genera. The *Accipiter* genus and the *Buteo* genus include many hawks common to North America.

Length: Hawks may be 10 to 27 inches (25 to 69 centimeters) long.

Weight: Hawks may weigh from .2 to 3 pounds (.1 to 1.4 kilograms).

Appearance: Most hawks are a shade of brown or blue-gray. Some are nearly white or solid black. Hawks usually have an underbelly that is a lighter shade than their back.

Hawks

Life span: Hawks can live between 10 and 30 years. Larger birds often live longer than smaller birds.

Habitat: Hawks live on all the continents except Antarctica. They live in various habitats. These areas include forests, mountains, rain forests, prairies, marshlands, savannas, tundra, and deserts.

Prey: Hawks eat other birds such as songbirds and crows. They hunt small mammals such as rabbits, mice, and squirrels. They also may eat frogs, snakes, and insects.

In This Chapter:

* Hawks are birds of prey.

* Eagles, some vultures, and hawks are related.

* Accipiters and buteos are two types of hawks.

Chapter 1

Hawks

Hawks are birds of prey. They hunt other animals for food. They often swoop down from great heights to catch prey on the ground. People have recorded a hawk diving toward prey as fast as 168 miles (270 kilometers) per hour.

Birds of prey are called raptors. This word comes from a Latin word which means "to catch and carry off." After catching prey, raptors often carry it to a safe place to eat. Hawks, eagles, vultures, owls, and falcons are raptors.

Birds of Prey

Hawks are members of the Accipitridae family. Eagles, kites, and some vultures also belong to this scientific group. These birds have similar features. They have excellent eyesight, sharp claws, and hooked beaks.

Scientists further divide hawks into closely related groups called genera. The *Accipiter* and the *Buteo* genera include hawks common in North America.

Hawk Species

About 22 hawk species live in North America. A species is a specific type of animal. Northern goshawks, Cooper's hawks, and sharp-shinned hawks live in North America. Broad-winged hawks, Swainson's hawks, and red-tailed hawks also are common in North America.

Types of Hawks

Some hawks are called accipiters. These hawks have bodies designed for chasing birds. Accipiters have short, round wings and a long tail. Their body shape helps them twist and turn quickly as they fly.

Buteo hawks glide on air currents.

Buteo hawks are soaring hawks. Their body shape helps them glide on air currents. Buteos have broad wings and a short, fan-shaped tail. They actually flap their wings only occasionally as they soar. They can glide for hours while searching for prey.

Many hawks nest in trees.

Appearance

Hawks vary in color. Most are either a shade
of brown or blue-gray. Some may be nearly
white. Others are almost solid black. Hawks
may have speckled or streaked feathers. Hawks
usually have a dark back and a lighter colored
underbelly.

Hawk species vary in size. Some hawks may only be 10 inches (25 centimeters) long. These hawks may weigh only .2 pound (.1 kilogram). Larger hawks may be up to 27 inches (69 centimeters) long and may weigh 3 pounds (1.4 kilograms). Female hawks usually are larger than males.

Young

Hawks mate in late spring or early summer. Female hawks then lay between one and six eggs. Larger hawk species usually lay fewer eggs. The eggs hatch in about 25 to 35 days.

Young hawks grow quickly. They can leave the nest in as few as 30 days after hatching. But they often stay with their parents for several more weeks to learn how to hunt.

Nesting

Most hawk species nest in trees. They may build nests from twigs, grasses, and other plant materials. Some hawks nest in grassy areas on the ground. A few hawk species nest on cliff ledges. Others use old nests left by other birds.

In This Chapter:

* Accipiter hawks hunt mostly birds.

* Buteo hawks are soaring hawks.

* Hawks have excellent vision.

Chapter 2

The Hunt

Hawks hunt many types of prey. Some hawks eat mostly other birds such as songbirds or crows. Other hawks eat small mammals such as rabbits, mice, and squirrels. Hawks also feed on frogs, snakes, and insects. They even eat dead animal flesh called carrion.

Accipiter Hunting Methods

Different hawk species use different methods to hunt. Northern goshawks, Cooper's hawks, and other accipiters ambush their prey. They may hide in the shadows on a tree branch. When a bird flies by, they burst out from their hiding spot to chase it.

Some accipiters fly low to the ground as they look for prey.

Accipiters dart and zigzag between trees as they chase prey. Their long tail helps them quickly change directions while flying. They match every move their prey makes. They then grab it out of the air as it is flying.

Some accipiters sneak up on their prey. They may fly low to the ground looking for prey.

They use trees, bushes, stumps, and dips in the ground to hide as they fly.

An accipiter may even flush birds out of a bush. The hawk flies straight toward a bush. This action scares birds hiding in the bush. The hawk then tries to catch birds that flee out the other side of the bush.

Buteo Hunting Methods

Buteo hawks soar high in the sky. They can glide on air currents for hours as they search for prey. Buteo hawks often hunt for small mammals and reptiles.

Buteos soar over fields and canyons until they spot prey below. To catch an animal, they dive toward it at a great speed.

Hunting

Some buteos sit on a perch and wait for prey to pass beneath them. They then swoop down on the prey. A few hawks walk along the ground to catch insects, snakes, and lizards.

Hawks have binocular vision.

Sight

Hawks have excellent vision. A hawk can see a mouse from 300 feet (90 meters) in the air.

Hawks see more shades of colors than people do. This ability helps hawks see animals that are almost the same color as their surroundings.

Hawks have binocular vision. Their eyes point forward. The field of vision from each eye overlaps. Binocular vision allows hawks to judge depth and distance. This ability is very important when hawks dive toward prey.

Hawks also can see about eight times more clearly than people can. A hawk's light-colored eyes have many special nerves and sensory cells. These nerves and cells allow hawks to focus on and follow fast-moving prey.

What Hawks Eat

Birds

Rabbits

Mice

Lizards

In This Chapter:

*   Hawks have sharp talons on their feet.

*   Some hawks defend a territory.

*   Hawks use their beaks to tear flesh from prey.

Chapter 3

The Kill

Hawks kill prey with their talons. These sharp claws are on the ends of their toes.

Hawks have four toes on each foot. Three toes point forward and one points backward. Hawks use their toes to grip branches as they perch. They also use their talons to grab prey.

Hawks have strong, sharp beaks. Their beaks are curved like a hook. Hawks use their beaks to tear flesh from prey.

Talons

The shape of a hawk's toes tells what it hunts. Accipiters have long, thin toes. Their talons are sharp and curved. This shape is good for catching birds.

Hawks that hunt birds usually catch them in midair. These hawks have long, slim legs and thin toes. They can reach out and grab prey quickly while flying. They rarely strike with great force. But they can easily hold their prey as they carry it away.

Buteos have fat legs, short toes, and thick talons. These features are better for hunting larger animals on the ground. Buteos can even catch prey close to their own size.

Hawks that hunt animals on the ground have strong leg

Territory

Some hawks defend a territory. This area may be where they nest or hunt.

A hawk may attack or threaten other predators that enter its territory. The hawk will raise the crest of feathers on its head. It may fly back and forth over its territory. It also may call out loudly to scare away other predators.

Hawks have sharp talons at the ends of their toes.

and feet muscles. They can kill prey by squeezing their talons around the animal.

Hawks can kill their prey quickly with their feet. Their sharp talons are deadly. Most hawks kill their prey by stabbing them with their talons.

Hawks often carry prey back to a perch to eat.

Eating Habits

Hawks eat their prey in different ways. They sometimes swallow insects and small prey whole. They may carry large prey back to a perch. They then use their beak to rip the prey's flesh into chunks. They swallow these chunks whole.

Hawks may swallow the bones, fur, or feathers of their prey. But they cannot digest all of these body parts. Hawks then vomit a mass of undigested food called a pellet or cast.

Hawks spend different amounts of time hunting. Hawks that eat small animals may hunt several times a day to find enough food. Hawks that hunt large prey do not hunt as often. They may get enough food from one kill to last for a day or two.

Myth: Hawks are cruel and kill other animals for no reason.

Fact: Hawks kill only when they are hungry. They are important and necessary to the balance of nature. They help keep prey animals from overpopulating an area.

Myth: Large birds of prey will swoop down and carry off small children.

Fact: There are no reported records of a bird of prey carrying off a child. In general, birds of prey seem to fear people. They also are not large enough to carry even a very small child.

In This Chapter:

* Hawks help control animal populations.

* Pollution can harm hawks.

* Laws protect birds of prey.

Chapter 4

In the World of People

People have mixed feelings about hawks and other raptors. For thousands of years, native peoples have respected and honored hawks for their speed and strength. They painted pictures of hawks and prayed to them. Today, people put pictures of hawks on flags, coins, and artwork.

But not everyone likes hawks. Some people believe hawks are cruel and harmful killers. Others do not like them because hawks sometimes kill songbirds. Some farmers dislike hawks because they think hawks will kill their chickens.

Yellow represents the hawk's range.

Importance of Hawks

Hawks are important to the balance of nature. They usually hunt animals that are plentiful. They help keep these animals from overpopulating an area. Hawks also hunt old, sick, and weak animals.

Hawks help farmers. Hawks eat mice, insects, and other farm pests. These animals may eat crops or spread diseases.

Some hawks eat dead animal flesh. This habit keeps diseases in rotting flesh from spreading to other animals.

Threats to Hawks

Pollution is a danger to hawks. People use chemicals called pesticides on plants. These chemicals kill insects that harm crops. Some prey animals eat the insects or plants sprayed with these chemicals. Predators then eat the prey animals. In this way, the chemicals can pass from plants and insects to hawks. The chemicals may kill hawks. They also may cause hawks to lay eggs with thin shells. These eggs will not hatch.

Many hawks die by accident. Some fly into buildings, power lines, or radio towers. Cars may hit raptors eating carrion on the road.

Habitat Loss

The worst threat to hawks is the loss of their habitat. People cut down forests to build homes. This practice destroys hawk nesting sites. Hawks in these areas might not breed. They then could die out.

Scientists' Concerns

Scientists have a difficult time counting hawks and other raptors. Hawks live in many areas. Their numbers may go up and down a great deal. In many areas, scientists believe that hawks are not in danger of dying out.

But scientists still are concerned about hawk populations. Countries in North America and Europe banned the use of pesticides such as DDT. Hawk populations then increased in these countries. But countries in other parts of the world still use harmful chemicals. Many countries also clear land and destroy hawk habitats. Some hawks are in danger of dying out in these areas.

People are working hard to protect all raptors. Laws in North America and Europe protect birds of prey. In these places, it is illegal to capture or kill a hawk without a permit.

Wildlife parks and organizations study and learn about different hawk species. Workers at these places set up programs to teach people about raptors. Their efforts are helping to save birds in many areas.

Many countries have laws that help protect hawks.

accipiter (ak-SIH-puh-tur)—a woodland hawk; accipiter hawks usually hunt birds.

buteo (BYOO-tee-oh)—a soaring hawk; buteo hawks usually hunt animals that are on the ground

carrion (KARE-ee-uhn)—dead animal flesh

habitat (HAB-uh-tat)—the place and natural conditions in which plants and animals live

pellet (PEL-it)—a mass of undigested hair, fur, and bones vomited up by a hawk

pesticide (PESS-tuh-side)—a chemical used to kill pests such as insects

predator (PRED-uh-tur)—an animal that hunts other animals for food

raptor (RAP-tur)—a bird of prey

talon (TAL-uhn)—a hawk's sharp claw

To Learn More

Collard, Sneed B. *Birds of Prey: A Look at Daytime Raptors.* Watts Library. New York: Franklin Watts, 1999.

Kalman, Bobbie. *Raptors.* Birds Up Close. New York: Crabtree Publishing, 1998.

Kops, Deborah. *Hawks.* Wild Birds of Prey. Woodbridge, Conn.: Blackbirch Press, 2000.

Sharth, Sharon. *Hawks.* Chanhassen, Minn.: Child's World, 2001.

Useful Addresses

Alberta Birds of Prey Centre
P.O. Box 1150
Coaldale, AB T1M 1M9
Canada

**American Museum of
    Natural History**
Central Park West at 79th
    Street
New York, NY 10024-5192

Hawk Mountain Sanctuary
1700 Hawk Mountain Road
Kempton, PA 19529-9449

The Raptor Center
University of Minnesota
Gabbert Raptor Building
1920 Fitch Avenue
St. Paul, MN 55108

Internet Sites

Diurnal Birds of Prey

http://www.seaworld.org/infobooks/Raptors/
   home.html

GeoZoo Birds—Day Raptors

http://www.geobop.com/Birds/Falconiformes

The Raptor Center

http://www.raptor.cvm.umn.edu

Index